CW01638102

THI

BOBBY CONNER

Edited by Frank A. DeCenso Jr.

DESTINY IMAGE PUBLISHERS

Scripture is the authors' own. Please note that Destiny Image's publishing style capitalizes certain pronouns in Scripture that refer to the Father, Son, and Holy Spirit, and may differ from some publishers' styles. Take note that the name satan and related names are not capitalized. We choose not to acknowledge him, even to the point of violating grammatical rules.

DESTINY IMAGE® PUBLISHERS, INC.

P.O. Box 310, Shippensburg, PA 17257-0310

"Speaking to the Purposes of God for this Generation and for the Generations to Come."

This book and all other Destiny Image, Revival Press, Mercy Place, Fresh Bread, Destiny Image Fiction, and Treasure House books are available at Christian bookstores and distributors worldwide.

For a U.S. bookstore nearest you, call 1-800-722-6774.

For more information on international availability, call 717-532-3040.

Reach us on the Internet at www.destinyimage.com.

Digital Edition ISBN: 978-0-7684-1977-1

Trade Paper ISBN: 978-0-7684-1976-4

Originally published in *Amazed by the Power of God*, ISBN 978-0-7684-2755-4.

The Real Supernatural

Bobby Conner

In Whom I Am Well-Pleased

Nothing could be more satisfying than knowing that your life is pleasing to God and hearing, "This is my beloved child in whom I am well pleased!"

The Lord is looking for a people whose heart is upright with Him, so that He can fully support all that they are doing see (see 2 Chron. 16:9). The Spirit of Truth is raising up leaders that will teach the people the vast difference between what is pure and what is profane (see Ezek. 44:23). It is crucial that we walk in uprightness if we are to ascend the hill of the Lord (see Ps. 24:3-4). It is very important that we do whatever needs to be done to walk in true authority. However, there is something more needful than just *ascending* into the hill of the Lord—that is *abiding* in the hill or presence of the Lord (see Ps. 15:1).

The Body of Christ must advance from just visitation to habitation (see Eph. 2:20-22). It is one thing to display the *power of God* but is so much better to reveal the *person of Christ.* As we embrace accountability, we can then be trusted with more true authority. Christ Jesus informed us that if we are faithful over little, we will become ruler over much more (see Matt. 25:14-21). On the other hand, if we fail to handle small things correctly, even the small things are in danger of being removed (see Matt. 25:24-29). It is required of a steward that he be found faithful (see 1 Cor. 4:2). Our goal is to live in such a manner that when we stand before the Lord He will say well done good and faithful servant. These days call for the highest standard of leadership.

The message of the Book of Jude is blasting out to this end-time Church age. The warning is all too clear: If we do not return to the acts of the apostles, we will continue to see the actions of the apostates. It is imperative that we become contenders and defenders of the faith, and "...contend for the faith that was once for all entrusted to the saints" (Jude 3).

In a vivid prophetic experience the Spirit of the Lord spoke these encouraging words to me, *"Accept no imitations! Expect no limitations! Embrace infinite possibilities!"* As we aspire to make these three areas a living reality in our lives, we will see the Church being launched into a much higher level.

Accept No Imitations

Artificial, counterfeit, synthetic—these are but a few words that help us grasp a better understanding of the word *imitation.* I once asked the president of a leading bank, "How do your tellers detect a counterfeit bill?" His answer was profound, "The best way to expose phony money is to have someone who is so accustomed to handling the real thing that when they touch a fake, something within them instantly sets off a warning."

This is what the Body of Christ must have: True intimacy with Jesus that instantly reveals any imitation. We must become so accustomed to His voice that we are not moved by the enticing of a stranger's voice. If we are the sheep of His fold, we must come to know His voice, and follow the voice of our Shepherd. We cannot continue to spend our lives on that which is worthless. Everything that is wood, hay, and stubble must be removed from our Christian walk.

It is crucial for the Church to commence walking in true apostolic authority. However, if we are going to be trusted with a higher level of authority it is essential for us to walk in integrity and uprightness. The writer of the Book of Hebrews instructs us to pursue peace as well as purity for without it we will not see the Lord.

The Lord spoke these encouraging words to me, *"If I can find a people without mixture, I will pour out My power without measure."* According to the Book of Revelation, there will emerge a group of "overcomers" walking in true Kingdom power. This causes three questions to arise in my heart: *If not you, who? If not here, where? If not now, when?*

The Zadok Priesthood

I was recently in the Northwest region of the United States and it suddenly began to rain the most wonderful sweet, steady rain seemingly from a cloudless sky. I asked the Lord, "What is this rain a sign of?" In response, I heard within my spirit, *"The substantial rainfall signified the anointed teaching that is being released through the emerging Zadok priesthood."* These anointed priests will begin to authenticate that which is holy and expose that which is profane. This is what the Lord called the Zadok priesthood to do: "Moreover, they shall teach My people the difference between the holy and the profane, and cause them to discern between the unclean and the clean" (Ezek. 44:23 NASB). What is the difference between the profane and the holy? The Lord said what He called profane was anything we are doing that He did not initiate. Remember the words of Christ Jesus when He states, "I never knew you, depart from Me you who practice lawlessness" (Matt. 7:23). These words were spoken to a person who had been very involved in religious activity, but did not truly trust Christ.

The fundamental purpose of the Zadok priesthood is to minister to the Lord as described in Ezekiel 44:15-16:

> *"But the priests, the Levites, the sons of Zadok, who kept charge of My sanctuary when the children of Israel went astray from Me, they shall come near Me to minister to Me; and they shall stand before Me to offer Me the fat and the blood," says the Lord God. "They shall enter My sanctuary, and they shall come near My table to minister to Me, and they shall keep My charge."*

This signifies an emphasis on the fivefold ministry of prophetic teachers as they prepare the Body of Christ to receive the strong prophetic and apostolic ministries yet to be truly inaugurated.

TEACHING THE TRUTH

The Spirit of Truth is seeking to establish each one of us in truth. Christ Jesus commanded, "Sanctify them by Your truth; Your word is truth" (John 17:17). As believers, we are to have upright lives which are characterized by authentic lifestyles of faith. Our walk must match our talk if we are to have a message that will legitimately change lives. It is time to take a stand for righteousness and holiness.

Grace is not a license to live loose. In our attempts to appear politically correct, have we drifted far from the calling to stand for truth and righteousness? Only as we return to true holiness of heart can we be vessels of honor. This will allow us to be sanctified in truth and be presentable to the Lord as consecrated vessels. The call is clear. We must present the truth in order for true freedom to reign in our hearts. God is calling each of us to embrace the conditions of Second Corinthians 7:1, "Therefore, having these promises, beloved, let us cleanse ourselves from all filthiness of the flesh and spirit, perfecting holiness in the fear of God."

Many feel a sense of disorientation at this time; this is the result of being upon the "Potter's wheel." However, be assured the Master Potter Himself is about to touch the soft pliable clay, and soon we will bear His image. We are in a time of transition that will produce transformation. Our responsibility is to remain soft and moist—yielded upon the Master's wheel. If we attempt to mold ourselves or if we allow ourselves to become dry and brittle we must be broken and remolded. It is imperative that we stay soft and surrendered before the Lord.

CHARACTER—NOT JUST GIFTINGS

Presently these emerging leaders are in a season of sifting and pruning—the refiner's fire is forging their character to carry this unique anointing. They will be the leaders and counselors who will not judge by what their eyes see nor what their ears hear, but in true righteousness they will make decisions resulting in equity and justice.

The refiner's fire is absolutely purifying these leaders so the anointing will not be lost nor the wineskins damaged or destroyed for lack of character. It will be a true impartation of the divine nature and holy character established in the spirit and soul of the Lord's leadership.

As our character is formed upon the Potter's wheel and through the Refiner's fire, it is imperative that we do not forget the wonderful promise given by the Spirit of God, *"If I can find a people without mixture, I will pour out My power without measure."* Again, let me impress upon each of us the mandate to embrace the promise of purity found in Second Corinthians 7:1, "Therefore, having these promises, beloved, let us cleanse ourselves from all filthiness of the flesh and spirit, perfecting holiness in the fear of God." The results of this embrace will be the identifying of us as sons and daughters of the almighty God. What an awesome motivation for purity.

The Spirit of Truth is calling for each of us to walk as it did the true Zadok priests. These priests had the responsibility of modeling and maintaining the highest standards of morality, self-control, and self-denial. They were charged with the ministry of teaching the people how to distinguish between what was godly and ungodly, so no deception would lead the people away from the Lord.

We must remember that there is a vast difference between deception and denial. Many today are actually walking in deception because they do not know that they have departed from the true path of righteousness. Those who embrace the call to the Zadok priesthood will be used by God to unveil their deception. However, many are also aware of their wanderings, but choose to walk in denial of the fact that they have turned away from their first love. Only those who deal with any and every way that their allegiance to Christ is artificial, and become genuine, authentic, and unadulterated in their walk with Him will inherit the powerful and precious promises God is pouring out to His end-times Church.

Expect No Limitations

In Scripture the question is posed, "Is there anything too hard for the Lord?" (Gen. 18:14). The prophet Jeremiah answers this question clearly: "Ah, Lord God! Behold, You have made the heavens and the earth by Your great power and outstretched arm. There is nothing too hard for You" (Jer. 32:17). The cry of our soul must be: "God, nothing is impossible with You!" If we would expect more, I am sure God would release more. According unto your faith be it unto you. Let's pray for big faith that moves the hand of God. Now is the time to think big, God can do anything. It is time to expect more, believe for more, and ask for more. Paul the apostle reminded us that, God "is able to do exceeding abundantly above all we could ask or think according to the power that works in us" (Eph. 3:20-21).

The following are some faith-building statements from saints of yesterday:

There are boundless possibilities for us, if we dare to act in God and dare to believe.

—SMITH WIGGLESWORTH

The only limit to the power of God lies within the individual.

—KATHRYN KUHLMAN

It is when active faith dares to believe God to the point of action that something has to happen.

—Kathryn Kuhlman

Embrace Infinite Possibilities

In order to embrace someone we must seek to draw near, reaching forth our hand, taking hold of them, and bringing them near to our heart. A true embrace is heart to heart; there is no such thing as a distant embrace. We cannot embrace this coming move of God from a distance. He is calling each of us to draw nearer to Him. It is time to come aside to know His heart. In Psalm 46:10 we are instructed to be still and know that He is the Lord. It is only as we behold His face that we are truly changed into His divine image. So I encourage you to meditate upon these promises. If we will accept no imitation and walk in unadulterated union with Christ, all the while seeking to have an indisputable relationship with Christ Jesus, then we can expect no limitations. It is time now to begin to embrace the formation of a character within us that will release God's infinite possibilities.

As believers we are instructed to live our daily lives with true goals, aims, and divine purpose. We cannot achieve this unless we walk in God's grace.

God is not looking for strong people to help Him accomplish His work. The

Lord is looking for people who are weak enough to be used. We must remember that His strength is made perfect in our weakness (see 2 Cor. 12:9). The key to experiencing supernatural liberating strength is personal weakness. Now let me make it clear that I am not speaking about weak character, or being weak in knowing the Scriptures. I am talking about a people who have come to the place where they have lost confidence in the power of the flesh to accomplish the work of the Spirit. It is at this point when we become strong and "graced" to accomplish things for the true advancing of God's glorious Kingdom.

This truth is clearly displayed in the story found in Psalm 107:23-28 of the strong, seaworthy sailors who made their living upon the high seas. However, one day the Lord raised up a stormy wind that blew away all their self-confidence. They found themselves at their wit's end. It was at this point that they cried out for the Lord's grace and help. Though they were skilled and experienced, the winds and waves of the sea convinced them of their dependence upon God. Have you encountered the winds of change in your life? If not, you can be confident they are on their way, in order to test your foundation.

Christ Jesus declares "without Me you can accomplish nothing!" (John 15:5). The word *nothing* means: "completely, totally nothing." It truly means less than nothing. It is a life of joy when we come to the place where we understand that it must be the work of the Spirit to advance the Kingdom of God.

Absolutely nothing you have ever done, nothing you could ever accomplish, will match the unparalleled joy of allowing Jesus to live His life through you. God has exactly fitted for each of us a unique walk of grace. As we yield our wills and ways to the control of God's Holy Spirit, we begin to experience the walk of grace. In this arena, you will experience the abundant grace that enables you to accomplish all that God has assigned you to do.

This deposit of grace is what makes the fire of passion burn so brightly in new believers. One of the great joys of pastoring people for years was the overwhelming joy of watching a new believer express with excitement the new things God was doing in their lives. The joy and excitement of new believers are contagious. It is extremely refreshing to be around brand-new believers; their entire life is ablaze with the love of God. As pastor, I was able to teach a new converts' class, and my heart was always blessed by the joy that Jesus Christ produced in the life of a new believer. It is this grace that causes the light of contentment to dance in the eyes of mature believers who have learned the secret of walking the grace walk. Our lives should testify to the ability of God's awesome grace to use us to accomplish great and mighty things for the glory of God.

You cannot separate life's actions from a grace-filled life. We are saved by grace, and we are kept by God's awesome grace. The Body of Christ seems to understand much concerning the grace of God touching an unbeliever's life, and bringing that person into a place of salvation. However, we lack true understanding concerning the ability of God's grace to operate in the daily lives of believers, thereby bringing them into a place of true effectiveness and fruitfulness. Grace does not just change your mind. It has a transforming effect upon your life. Grace is a powerful motivator provoking us to reach higher and accomplish more for Christ and His Kingdom.

Essential Ingredients for Grace

The apostle Paul stated in First Corinthians 15:10, "But by the grace of God I am what I am, and His grace toward me was not in vain; but I labored more abundantly than they all, yet not I, but the grace of God which was with me." Paul declared that the grace of God was not wasted upon his life, but he labored more because of the grace active in his life. Though all we are and all we do are because of God's grace, we are still called to labor abundantly to advance His

Kingdom. One of the great paradoxes of the Christian life is that it is only by and through grace that we accomplish anything, yet God expects us to labor diligently in His service. Charles Spurgeon said, *"Faith goes up the stairs that love has built and looks out the window which hope has opened."*

Just as diligent labor is required to extract out all of the grace that God has given us, humility is required to obtain grace. "All of you, clothe yourselves with humility toward one another, because, 'God opposes the proud, but gives grace to the humble'" (1 Pet. 5:5 NASB). Grace is promised to the humble. A great saint of years by gone, Walter Buettler, made this observation—*"the moment humility announces herself she is already on her way out the door."* If we would be truly humble, and careful not to touch the glory of God, always giving Him praise for what He is doing, I am sure we would receive more grace. The Lord warned me once that the highest form of treason was to take the gifts and graces He has given leadership to win and woo the Bride to Himself, and then use these gifts and graces to win the Bride to ourselves.

May each heart embrace the promise given in Psalm 84:11 (NASB), "For the Lord God is a sun and shield; the Lord gives grace and glory..." In this passage we see the true key to the advancing of the Kingdom of God. It is by God's gift of grace that we are able to behold the glory. Any good thing ever accomplished by humankind is the direct result of the anointing and impartation of God's grace. May we walk a grace-filled life in order to see the glory of God fill the earth.

Grace is an open door that bids us to draw nearer to God. In Proverbs 8:17,21, God declares, "I love those who love Me, and those who seek Me diligently will find Me.... That I may cause those who love Me to inherit wealth, that I may fill their treasuries." Now this is an awesome promise and powerful incentive, finding

God and having Him bless us with overflowing treasures. We must never forget that God has great plans for His people. Hear His promise in Jeremiah 29:11, "For I know the thoughts that I think toward you, says the Lord, thoughts of peace, and not of evil, to give you a future and a hope." It is time to open our hearts wide to the grace of God. He is a good God and has great plans for each of us.

Waiting Upon God

The Lord desires to change us. He seeks to bring us up into His purpose for us. He waits for us to reach out to Him and knock on the door of His heart. Just as Esther had to approach the throne of her husband, we too must prepare ourselves to approach the throne of God. He, too, has extended His scepter. Now is the time grace has provided an open door in Heaven. It is time to approach the throne of God's grace to find favor and help during these days.

Spending quiet time in the Lord's presence is tremendous, and carries great importance. It is as we wait upon Him that we are renewed in power and strength (see Isa. 40:28-31). Each of us must find a special quiet place where we can shut out the cares of this world and get alone with God. Each day we should come within our "set apart place" to worship, acknowledge His goodness and grace concerning us, and thank Him for His guidance and blessing upon our lives. Great grace is released when we truly enter His gates with thanksgiving and into His courts with praise by taking the time to praise the Lord and to bless His holy name.

As we take time to behold Him with an unveiled face, we are changed into ever-increasing glory. In this place of quiet worship and prayerful reading of His holy Word, there is a release of grace producing "Spirit and Life" which flows into our being to build our faith and provide the "enabling grace" for obedience. It is essential that we set apart time each day to be in His presence. Being part of a local church and attending church services are essential and not to be neglected, but this is no substitute for our devotional times alone with the Lord of glory.

Being One With the Lord

Notice in Luke 3:2 that the Word of God came to John while he was alone in the wilderness. The programs of the "church" of that day were in full operation, yet John was called apart to be with the Lord alone. So also today, there are those who are spiritually hungry and seeking something more, who likewise are being called apart to be alone with the Lord for a time of preparation. As a result of his being alone with the Lord, John came into a oneness with the Lord that could not have been accomplished in any other way.

When John was asked who he was, his response testifies to this experience. He said, "I am the voice of one crying in the wilderness 'Make straight the way of the Lord,' as the prophet Isaiah said" (John 1:23). Each one of us should come to the place where we also could make this statement: "I am the voice of One." There is an urgent need for this "voice" to cry out in the midst of the frustrations and perils of our present day. We live in a world that must have the grace and peace of God.

The need today is not newfangled methodology, but rather a turning aside to stand in the manifest presence of the Lord to be prepared as "the voice of one crying in the wilderness" of our day. May it be stated of us, as it was of the disciples of old, that it is apparent that we have been with Jesus. This and only this will make the changes that must occur if we are to reach this hurting world with the message of God's redemptive transforming grace.

Toward the end of his life, a popular minister was asked what he would do if he had his life to live over again. He said he had spent seven years in preparation for 45 years of ministry. Instead, he would spend 45 years in preparation for seven years of ministry. It is very important how we begin, but it is far more important how we end.

The Lord is seeking to bring us to the end of our abilities so we can tap into His ability. This requires that we recognize His presence and turn aside to stand before Him. Only then will we become the expression of His voice—crying in the wilderness of our day.

God Values Your Friendship

The world we live in is extremely fast paced. Computers, iPods, cell phones, voice mail, e-mail, instant messaging, and other high-tech gadgets seem to leave very little opportunity for really getting to know people and developing true, lasting friendships.

In our busy world it is tragic to admit that many times it is the most important of these relationships, our companionship with Christ, that suffers the most. The Spirit of God calls each of us to turn aside from the cares and chaos of this world and come to Him for true companionship and friendship.

Maintaining True Friendship

As followers of Christ, even in the midst of a civilization that seems to shun true friendship we must never forget that we have a true Friend in "high places." This true Friend is the Son of God, Christ the Lord. He is a True Friend that remains closer than a brother. We could have no higher position than to be known as a true friend of God.

The most contented people in the world are those who have found Jesus

Christ to be life's truest Friend. A true friend is one who is always there for you. You can confide the deepest secrets of your heart with a dear, trusted friend. God also shares His secrets with His trusted Friends. Jesus promised in John 15:15: "No longer do I call you servants, for a servant does not know what his master is doing; but I have called you friends, for all things that I heard from My Father I have made known to you." The happiest people on earth are those who have surrendered control of their lives to the Spirit of God and entered into this friendship. The songwriter of old said it well, "What a friend we have in Jesus..."!

VALUE AND WORTH

God Himself highly values not only His friendship with you, but you His friend. The Lord has ascribed to you great worth. Countless numbers of Christians have never stopped to ponder the great value that God has placed upon their lives. It is almost overwhelming to consider the fact that almighty God has chosen you to become the eternal companion of His dear Son!

Can you imagine that, with the entire universe under His control and care, Father God actually delights and takes pleasure in fellowshipping with you? Truly you are extremely special to God. Knowing this, you should never be plagued with thoughts of unworthiness, feeling that your life has no true meaning or purpose. Christ would have done all that He did in coming to earth and dying on the cross if you were the only one on earth that needed redemption. That is how special you are to God! Heaven places great worth and value upon you. You are incredibly special to God.

How do we ascertain what something is worth? What determines the value of something? The answer: what someone is willing to pay for it. Think about it. God was willing to give Heaven's best—His own Son—to redeem you. That shows your true worth and reveals your eternal value. Never again allow the enemy to make you feel like you don't have any real worth.

The Creator of the entire universe desires that you be in His presence for all eternity. There is no need to suffer in despair and loneliness when Christ reaches out to each of us and offers true love and friendship.

LIVING WITH PURPOSE— NOT STARDOM

As we daily continue walking in friendship and union with Christ, Scripture states that we walk in the light as He is in the light, and we have fellowship with one another. "But if we walk in the light as He is in the light, we have fellowship with one another, and the blood of Jesus Christ His Son cleanses us from all sin" (1 John 1:7). This is where our cleansing, contentment, and comradeship stem from: union with

Christ. As we abide in Him, our life finds its purpose and pleasure.

The most confident people on the face of the earth are Christians who are totally yielded to the control of the Spirit of God. Knowing that God has good plans for our lives, we are called to be living with a divine goal, aim, and purpose. "See then that you walk circumspectly, not as fools but as wise, redeeming the time, because the days are evil. Therefore do not be unwise, but understand what the will of the Lord is" (Eph. 5:15-17). We should be living in a wise and worthy manner, which means following the plan for which God gave us life. To truly accomplish this we must be guided daily by the Holy Spirit. When we live in such a way, we will find our lives are the most fulfilled.

Now is the time for the history makers to emerge and take their place. The Spirit of Truth is erasing a huge lie that has paralyzed the Body of Christ, which says God only uses the "superstar saint." Nothing could be farther from biblical truth. God uses ordinary people to accomplish extraordinary exploits. Remember, the promise of Isaiah 40:31 is for all who hope in the Lord: "But those who hope in the Lord will renew their strength. They will soar on wings like eagles; they will run and not grow weary, they will walk and not be faint" (NIV).

The Preparation of Friendship

The Spirit of God has chosen you to live during these important days in history. Each of us should strive to accomplish great things for the glory of God. The greatest achievement we are called to is a continuing companionship and friendship with Christ. As we walk in this, we will become overcomers.

Our friendship with Christ helps prepare us for the harvest. The Church must be equipped to handle the coming waves of people. The masses of people that are coming will be from every walk and every level of society. Nothing can qualify us for this gathering of the harvest more quickly than friendship with Christ. It is only as the world takes notice that we have been with Christ that our witness will ring true.

This is what the leaders in Jerusalem said about Peter and John. "When they saw the courage of Peter and John, and realized that they were unschooled, ordinary men, they were astonished and they took note that these men had been with Jesus" (Acts 4:13). May the same be said about us; may the world see us as those who not only know *about* Christ, but *know* Him and are known *by* Him.

I have experienced the outstanding privilege of being in ministry meetings when suddenly the entire room is filled with the overwhelming smell of fresh baked bread. In most cases when this occurs we experience marvelous manifestations of divine healing. Jesus states that healing is the children's bread (see Mark 7:27). This bread for the sick and hurting is the Lord Jesus serving the bread of His presence, for He is the Healer. The Holy Spirit is releasing an awesome anointing for healing in our day; this anointing is going to be placed upon the Body of Christ.

In a prophetic visitation the Lord said to me, *"Tell the Church, ready or not here I come, and I have a gift in My hand... it is the gift of healing... it will be placed upon the Body not just upon somebody."* We have witnessed the marvelous gift of healing move and minister while resting upon somebody. For example Benny Hinn moves in an awesome gift of healing and miracles. This is wonderful, and we so appreciate all God is doing through this wonderful man of God; however what is coming will be far more awesome—a powerful anointing of healing and mighty miracles moving upon the entire Body of believers.

Many years ago, I was sent by the Lord to prophesy to Benny Hinn, tell-ing him that soon there would come a day when children would be moving in the power and anointing he is walking in. I will never forget his response. His eyes danced and sparkled as he said with absolute joy, *"Bobby, I know, the Lord has also told me that!"* Let us pray for that day to fall upon us now.

We stand on the very verge of the largest healing movement in the history of the Church. One of the reasons this healing anointing is coming is that we are going to need it. It is time to pray for Heaven's bread to be served in our meetings, offering prayer for the sick, anointing with oil, praying the prayer of faith, and expecting the Lord to manifest

Himself as the Bread of Heaven given for our healing.

Bread for the Sinful and Hungry

In Exodus 16, God answered the cry of His people for bread as they journeyed in the wilderness. This pure, white, round bread that God caused to rain down from Heaven upon His hungry people as they griped and grumbled about their wilderness walk, was a foreshadow or reflection of Christ Jesus. For example, sustenance came down from God out of Heaven; it was white, which speaks of purity; it was round, speaking of being endless, eternal. Christ declares that He is indeed the Bread sent down from Heaven. "I am the bread of life. He who comes to Me shall never hunger, and he who believes in Me shall never thirst" (John 6:35). How grateful we are to God for His wonderful provision of the Bread of Heaven. *Only as we receive and partake of Him do we have true life.* None need to starve or stumble in darkness, since we have been given the Light of the World and the true Bread of Life for our wilderness journey.

Sharing Heaven's Bread

It is time also to share the Bread of Heaven with hungry, hurting humanity. Our world is starving and desperate for Heaven's Bread—the Living Christ. There is a remarkable story recorded in the seventh chapter of Second Kings. Here we see people in the midst of a great famine. Never had there been such a desperate time. People were even stooping to cannibalism, eating their own children (see 2 Kings 6:25-29).

In the midst of such need, the prophetic word recorded in Second Kings 7:1 came to God's people. The prophet Elisha stood and declared boldly! "Hear the word of the Lord. Thus says the Lord, 'Tomorrow about this time a seah of fine flour shall be sold for a shekel, and two seahs of barley for a shekel, at the gate of Samaria.'" This is a bold prophetic statement. Right in the middle of this horrible famine, the prophet announces that on the next day there will be so much food available that it will almost be given away free.

We are instructed to trust in the Lord and we will be established, and to believe His prophets and we will prosper (see 2

Chron. 20:20). Notice the response of one of the not-so-wise leaders in Second Kings 7:2, who said in so many words that there is no way that even with God's intervention something like this could ever happen. To which Elisha replied, "...you will see it with your eyes, but you will not be one to take part in the provisions." You can see the outcome of this man's unbelief in Second Kings 7:17-19. He was trampled to death by the people rushing to eat of the food that God had provided. It is shocking and surprising how and who God used to provide such a mighty miracle. We must remember it is in our weakness that God's strength is made perfect, for when we are weak He is strong.

We must be like the four lepers in Second Kings 7:9. These pitiful, sick, dying men made a choice to change their situation. Asking the question, "Why sit here until we die?," they were compelled to get up and go forward, seeking a change. Can't you just see these four pitiful men with advanced leprosy as they stood upon their wounded feet that were infected and filled with painful sores? I can see them as they weakly stand, supporting each other as they attempt to steady their trembling bodies, limping off into the unknown, and knowing only that there must be more than what they are experiencing now.

What about you? Like the lepers, are you sick and tired of the lack of spiritual food? Are you ready to get up and advance into the unknown? Do you too need to ask yourself, "Am I going to sit here until I die?" We will never seek change if we are content with our situation.

As the lepers entered into the camp of the enemy soldiers who surrounded Jerusalem, they discovered it had been quickly and completely vacated. The enemy, in abject terror, had fled leaving behind not only the tables filled with wonderful bread and foods, but all their wealth. The question is how could four weak, pathetic lepers strike such terror and fear into the hearts of such a formidable foe? The answer is found in Second Kings 7:5-7. The Lord God had made the foe hear the sound of a mighty army advancing, bringing about these overwhelming results. When these four men entered the camp there was no opposition at all, only tables of food and tents filled with treasure. These starving men filled their stomachs full. Then they were filled with another hunger, the need to share what they had found with others. They were gripped with the understanding that they were responsible for sharing, with other starving people, the bread they had found.

For those of us to whom the Bread of Heaven has been given, we too must share Him with others. It is the cry of my heart that God will release outstanding grace for us to share Heaven's Bread with the hurting and hungry of the world. Amen!

> *My beloved spoke, and said to me: "Rise up, my love, my fair one, and come away"* (Song of Solomon 2:10).

Jesus Christ said "Follow Me, and I will make you...." The Lord Jesus is beckoning us as His beloved Bride to fully follow Him. The invitation is extended—it is now time to respond. It is time to lay down our plans and follow the Lord. Jesus states in Matthew 16:24-25, "If any man will come after Me, let him deny himself, and take up his cross, and *follow Me*. For whosoever will save his life shall lose it: and whosoever will lose his life for My sake shall find it" (KJV). Again in John 12:26 we hear Jesus informing His disciples, "If any man serve Me, let him *follow Me;* and where I am, there shall also My servant be: if any man serve Me, him will My Father honor" (KJV).

During these days of preparation, nothing is more crucial than being with Jesus, and His presence being with you. This was Moses' desperate cry to God: that His presence would be with His people. "...If Your Presence does not go with us, do not bring us up from here.

For how then will it be known that Your people and I have found grace in Your sight, except You go with us?" (Exod. 33:15-16). God delights in those who desire Him. It is those who seek after Him whom He chooses as His disciples.

It is easy to understand why God chose Joshua to be the leader after the death of Moses. The key is found in Exodus 33:11, "So the Lord spoke to Moses face to face, as a man speaks to his friend. And he would return to the camp, but his servant Joshua the son of Nun, a young man, did not depart from the tabernacle." Joshua loved being in the presence of God. Those who pursue the presence of God will find themselves following Christ and being formed into His disciples.

THE DEFINITION OF A DISCIPLE

Jesus' call to His disciples was to follow Him. But what exactly is a disciple? The New Testament word for "disciple" is the Greek word *mathetes*, which means "a learner." It comes from the root word *manthano*, which means "to learn." This word deals with doing, not just hearing. Being a disciple denotes having a belief that is accompanied by behavior. What we have learned is to change our attitude, which in turn changes our actions. You can say you believe something, but until what you believe changes your actions, you are just living in deception. So the word *disciple* denotes, "one who actively follows one's teaching." The "disciples" of Jesus.

A disciple is not only a *student*, but a *follower*; hence we are spoken of as imitators of our Teacher. Too many would-be disciples in our day are looking to classes instead of picking up their crosses. If we are students without becoming followers, we are in danger of becoming dead in spirit and bound in legalism. On the other hand, if we are followers without becoming true students, we are in danger of becoming superficial, shallow, cotton-candy Christians who cannot effect our world for Christ.

A total commitment is crucial if we are to fulfill the Great Commission. We are about to find out that well *done* is better than well *said*. It was never the plan of God to establish the Kingdom of God just by talking. It is going to take doing. "For the kingdom of God is not a matter of talk but of power" (1 Cor. 4:20 NIV). The revival came in Samaria when the people heard and saw the miracles Philip was doing. "And the multitudes with one accord heeded the things spoken by Philip, hearing and seeing the miracles which he did" (Acts 8:6). Notice the first verse of the Book of Acts, "The former account I made...of all that Jesus began both to *do* and *teach*." It is important to note that the Scriptures record what Jesus taught and did. We must be doers of the Word, and not just hearers of the Word. Otherwise we deceive ourselves. "But be doers of the word, and not hearers only, deceiving yourselves" (James 1:22).

CARPE DIEM—SEIZE THE DAY

It has been said, "We cannot direct the wind; however, we can adjust the sails," and the time has come for the Church to turn her sail to catch the wind of discipleship. We do not have time to waste; the only preparation for tomorrow is the right use of today. The Scriptures declare "... Behold, now is the accepted time..." (2 Cor. 6:2). It is time for the leaders in the Church to stop arguing about what a Christian is... and become one—a believing, following disciple of Christ! "... Be an example to the believers in word, in conduct, in love, in spirit, in faith, in purity" (1 Tim. 4:12). The coming leadership will be ordinary people with extraordinary determination—determination first and foremost to follow Jesus!

We have an open door to reach out with the gospel to hurting humanity. It is time we become disciples of Christ and not settle for being only believers in Him. We must stop fussing over what we don't agree on—and start sharing the good news of the gospel. Apostle Paul spoke about the importance of good doctrine, but he also said that if on some points you disagree, don't become divided. Instead, he exhorted us to keep walking out what we know while allowing God to make clear any apparent contradictions. "...And if on some point you think differently, that too God will make clear to you. Only let us live up to what we have already attained" (Phil. 3:15-16 NIV).

Marks of a Disciple

There is no need to wonder if we are disciples of Christ or not. Jesus clearly defined what His disciples would look like. First, He said, "If you abide in My word, you are My disciples indeed" (John 8:31). When we abide in Christ's word, we confirm that we are one of His disciples. We must be like trees planted by the deep rivers of God's Word to bring forth fruit that will remain.

Jesus also said that His disciples will be doers. Their understanding will bring action. They will be like a prized apple tree in September—bearing much fruit for the Kingdom. "By this My Father is glorified, that you bear much fruit; so you will be My disciples" (John 15:8). Remember, Jesus is looking for doers; those who will be fruit-filled and fruitful.

The greatest proof of our discipleship, however, will not be our dogmatic adherence to doctrine, or the great things we accomplish in the name of Jesus, but rather it will be our love one for another. "By this all will know that you are My disciples, if you have love for one another" (John 13:35). Let us choose to abide in His Word, press on to fruitfulness, and walk in His love so that we may truly be His disciples.

May God grant to each of us the grace to fully follow Him so that He can mold and make our lives into His image. "For whom He foreknew, He also predestined to be conformed to the image of His Son, that He might be the firstborn among many brethren" (Rom. 8:29).

ABOUT BOBBY CONNER

Bobby Conner has an extensive ministry background as a Southern Baptist pastor, and he ministers in a high level, proven prophetic anointing. He believes his calling is to equip the Body of Christ to hear and discern God's voice in these times. He is well-loved and best known the world over for his sensitivity to and leading of the Holy Spirit. Highly esteemed as an internationally acclaimed conference speaker, Bobby has ministered effectively to more than 45 foreign countries as well as in the United States for many years. Bobby has been ministering for more than 38 years, and averages speaking five times a week.

BOOKS BY BOBBY CONNER

GOD'S SUPERNATURAL POWER

NOTES

Printed in Great Britain
by Amazon

17305965R00061